PERPETUAL MOTION

Also by Marilyn McCabe
Rugged Means of Grace (chapbook)

PERPETUAL MOTION

poems by
Marilyn McCabe

HILARY THAM CAPITAL COLLECTION
Selected by Gray Jacobik

THE WORD WORKS
WASHINGTON, D.C.

FIRST EDITION   FIRST PRINTING
Perpetual Motion
Copyright © 2012 Marilyn McCabe

Reproduction of any part of this book in any form or by any means, electronic or mechanical, except when quoted in part for the purpose of review, must be with permission from the publisher in writing. Address inquiries to:

The Word Works
PO Box 42164
Washington, DC 20015

wordworksbooks.org
editor@wordworksbooks.org

Cover art: *Marks We Make* 2003 Robert and Shana ParkeHarrison
Used by permission of the artists
Author photograph: Kathy McGee
Book design: Susan Pearce

Lines in section two of *"Please remember me"* are from letters and journal entries quoted in *Madame Curie*, a biography by Eve Curie, trans. Vincent Sheean. NY: Doubleday, Doran & Co., 1938.

Library of Congress Catalog Number: 2011938037
International Standard Book Number: 978-0-915380-82-4

ACKNOWLEDGMENTS

Thanks to the publications where these poems first appeared:

"Ashes Ashes," *Cider Press Review*
"Burning Bush," "Enemy's the Friend," *Praxilla*
"Eve on the Edge," *Cream City Review*
"For, behold, the kingdom of God is within you," *Cortland Review*
"Eve, Looking Back" (as "How the Body Remembers"),, *Poetry Midwest*
"If Beauty Is Just the Beginning of Terror," *Nimrod*
"Origami," *Blueline*
"Refuting Buddha," *Runes*
"Thoughts on Systems Theory," *Rhino*

Many of these poems previously appeared in the chapbook *Rugged Means of Grace*, Finishing Line Press, 2011.

CONTENTS

I. CONSIDERING MAGRITTE — 11

1. (With a Grain of Sel)f-Portrait — 13
2. *L'homme du large* — 14
3. *Le mouvement perpétuel* — 15
4. Problems and Affinities — 16
5. *Entr'acte* — 17

II. WITH A GRAIN OF SEL — 19

The World Makes Me Anew — 21
If Beauty Is Just the Beginning of Terror — 22
Farm-to-market — 24
What Lingers Longest — 25
For, behold, the kingdom of God is within you — 26
Origami — 27
Eve on the Edge — 28
I'll Take the #8: An Ars Poetica — 29

III. L'HOMME DU LARGE — 31

Perseveration — 33
Ashes Ashes — 34
Guide to Home Birth — 35
Write Me a Letter — 36
Insomniac Thoughts on the Special Theory of Relativity — 37
Love and the Big Bang — 38
Please remember me — 39
The Orion Nebula — 42
Thoughts on Systems Theory — 43
Wasp Nest — 44

IV. LE MOUVEMENT PERPÉTUEL — 45

Found — 47
At Freeman's Farm — 48
Mimesis — 50
Afghani Pieta — 51
The Human Equation — 52
Enemy's the Friend — 54
Sunset Strip — 55
Root Systems — 56

V. PROBLEMS AND AFFINITIES — 57

Burning Bush — 59
Lost — 60
Psalm: It Is Dark — 61
Lac du Saint Sacrament — 62
Eve, Looking Back — 63
Hieroglyphs — 64
Within Without — 65
Ode to Nevelson in Spring — 66
Signs of Passerines — 67
A Matter of Spirit and Flesh — 68
Spring on Lacy Road — 69
Refuting Buddha — 70

VI. ENTR'ACTE — 71

Appointment With — 73
Memory of a Voyage (Magritte) — 74

ABOUT THE WORD WORKS — 76
ABOUT THE HILARY THAM CAPITAL COLLECTION — 77
ALSO FROM THE WORD WORKS — 78
ABOUT THE AUTHOR / ABOUT THE ARTISTS — 81

I. CONSIDERING MAGRITTE

1. (With a Grain of Sel)f-Portrait

A gaping hole
where face should
be an unripe apple

a void at the caged gut
disguised by a bird. If I
were to open

my eyes you'd see
only sky. What a body
wants:

a good hat
to keep it all in,
some wooden wings

to weather storms from
sea, some clouds to stuff
in holes like bread

so the darkness doesn't
show through. My brain-
's aflame,

my heart a paper
doily. That's
gonna burn. Burn.

2. L'homme du large

From out of dark surf they rose, the frog
men bearing aloft the many keys
they'd wrested from Poseidon (or
were they the old pins from hinges
of drowned submarines; but no,
we don't discard old hard-
ware). At any rate,
they jangled off
down the beach and we fell
back to sleep on sand packed hard
as pinewood box
board to the strains of "Take me home…"

3. *Le mouvement perpétuel*

My head's a ball.
I dress myself in multi-
syllables. High brow? Yes,
all that's left of the old hare-
brained circus act, back and forth
on my trapeze. I repeat myself.
Have I told you this?
Have I told you this before?

4. Problems and Affinities

A door is a hole: leaf
a tree: boulder mountain: man
his own death.
Q. How is the rain
like a cloud? A. Like a puddle's
like a buffalo: roaming, amorphous.
The problem of water
is that we are all water
but look so much like ground.
The problem of sky
is it looks like surface
but things fall off it all the time.

5. *Entr'acte*

Between acts we dismantle ourselves,
blow the spittle from our tongues,
empty our legs of bone debris
and attempt reduction by means of flame,
half-heartedly. It seems strange
to speak so plainly through grease-
paint, scratch so visibly
under our wigs as if we weren't bald
or balding, to chew Turkish delight
under incandescent light. It's not easy

here. We're ourselves in sheep's
clothing, naked in some veils,
repeating lines we thought we knew, slacklip-
staring at tattered copies of our scripts.
What's my line? What's the time?
We're neither here nor there.

•

II. WITH A GRAIN OF SEL

The World Makes Me Anew

> *"...that call'd Body is a portion of Soul discern'd by the five Senses..."*
> —*William Blake*

My hand is made by the chilly morning air,
solid slip of my black Bic,
my mouth by the sharp warmth of French roast, my nose
its humid soil scent. My face is shaped by sun
mottling through the bare catalpa;
but this midwinter light's not strong enough
to pull my nearsighted eyes to focus.
They are crafted by this tiny thatch
of words relentless in their lines.
My skin's composed by the *snick* of chickadee.
One ear is named by the cardinal's *chuck*,
the other slung by a siren.
The river mutters my blood
to the outermost edges of a body
that, now defined by wind in the cedars, hungers.

If Beauty Is Just the Beginning of Terror

That takes us to the dark heart
of things: who we are, are not,
what we do when we die. It stabs us
and our blood drips like days, the untold
hours of when we're here,
where we stop short and are gone:
like the way the wind came
one day after Dave died
in a flurry of bike and deer
and clouds built themselves
an empire and the trees
bowed down and roofs fled,
barns collapsed,
sewers spewed
and all was gray and green,
then gone too blue
and the ghastly sun
like an operating room lamp
on the glowing insides of the patient,
the place where no light should go.

Quiet. Take the soft heart
from the body streaked
blue, white, red,
cup it like a bird
in your mortal hand,
but it can't fly, as time does.
It only counts the minutes,
forgetting from one to the next
the passing of time. Every
beat is new, every
fresh pulse a surprise,
seeking the return, rich
and weary: the beautiful
blood.

Farm-to-market

Once I hauled myself up to the maw
of a haymow and lived inside a while,
half-wild and dreaming
of birds, milkweed pods.

Flies gathered round,
crawling up the barnboards, waking
on the warm days,
as we all respond to heat.

I took me to the farmer's mart, a half
a heart to sell. The barn burned down,
flies like sparks spilled into the swamp ditch.
I ask you, what's a home without some ash?

Sometimes the wind blows funny.
Some pods never move,
lie wet like baby birds in a dry husk,
a different kind of lovely.

What Lingers Longest

In the dingy car window: half a reflection of your face,
half the dead zone along the highway acrid thick with burning
oil from Sunoco's massive tanks, sour-
dough stench of Schmidt's brewery, scattered
ruin of Tinnicum swamp. You try to hold your breath.

Time runs out. You exhale
yourself foggy on the window, suck
in the fume of the Schuylkill Expressway,
draw circles in the fog, and the residue
sticks in your lungs and the inside of your nose

so now, no matter how sweet the lilac hedge
from the deck of your pretty cottage, cup
of expensive coffee, supple shoes you got in Rome,
it's still there in the mucous membranes and you
are always holding your breath, just a little.

For, behold, the kingdom of God is within you

Luke 17:21

Not what I expect.
The hills are easy: they please,
leaning sun-etched
peaks. There are flowers,
burgundy, indigo, trees
like towers
or fountains.
Light thick as clouds

muffle sun. Odd fogs drift,
scatter of hail, spatter of rain,
winds shift.
There are dark turns, rumble of far trains.
Marshy worm scent, and leaves, dry.
Departing birds; their high cry.

Origami

The way all flat things
can be folded and tucked,
turned inside out—
suddenly a crane, a frog, a bulbous
hassock: what resides
in things that seem so
definitively
what they are:
the way you cried, surprised,
that day
when we saw the jay
half-gnawed
as if the owl'd been disrupted
mid-dinner, it was
an awful mess
of feather and blood and
the split of tiny bones
that opened
in you, unfolded
something
that had been carefully rendered,
flattened something
elaborately manipulated
and you lay yourself
across the small carnage
like a shroud.

Eve on the Edge

I thought it was leaves taking flight, flock of
The last leaves, in fact, beech perhaps, they hang on
Too long, or aspen, yellow like that, sweep and begin to
Plunge, the last hope of the tree, taken by Thanksgiving's
Wind, because that's the way the wind is, willful like that,
Cruel. And they began, inevitably, to fall, ultimately and always
To fall, to settle and dim under the rain the thunder
Foretold. The poor scattered and gray things would be
Indistinguishable from earth, and I thought,
Yes, this is the way things go. I knew things
Then, how the world worked, my legs hanging
Over the precipice, the rock hard under me, the earth
Carved away, nothing under my feet but wind. All things
Pass, and dull in the passing, nothing is as bright
For as long as the heart wants, everything
Leaves. Every one. But I tell you, as I watched, as I
Watched the leaves they became before my eyes:
Goldfinch, the last of summer, rose and turned and scattered
Like risen leaves and this was the beginning, the beginning
Of some great migration or the last summer tale told wildly
Flung wildly into the wind, turning over the Kaaterskill. I know
Nothing. Nothing.

I'll Take the #8: An Ars Poetica

I want some of those of fricasseed chickens, and roosters,
with their gnarled and alarming toes in the snow.
Comfort me with tubers and lichen-skinned erratics,
with strange scat, thatched knobs like the porcupine's;
and gaps like the one between Adam and God.
Give me feet like a farmer's, mud wallowed
and corny, that stride through the barn
to the metal forge where I'll beat out horseshoes,
their honest u's. What ever happened to horehound?
I'll have some of that, and licorice whips
and palm-warmed Silly Putty with which
to stretch the face of Charlie Brown from frown
to mere grimace, and a tiny chain of fine gold
that whispers at a decibel only other precious
metals can hear. Start me a language of sump pumps
and organs that blear to life like a drunk for last call
and the Star-Spangled Banner, and some of those pipes
the Peruvians play on the street in their old wool blankets
and Nike sneaks. Shouldn't that stop me, finally,
from the preening and cautious crawl toward the gutter,
the last one, I mean, the one they dig by hand, or
is that only in the movies? We're all just
whistling Dixie. I can play a little of that tune.
Yeah, give me some of that, and tell me:
what do I owe you?

III. L'HOMME DU LARGE

Perseveration

I'm walking downtown under the ghost of a half moon in the day sky
and think, I'm on a planet circled by a moon surrounded
by other planets circled by other moons in a galaxy circling something
and surrounded by other galaxies circling, and I'm dizzy from it,
and wonder why we developed the consciousness to ask why
we developed the consciousness to ask why we developed
that consciousness, and if our brain has a center whose tendency
is toward believing in a higher power does that disprove the existence of God,
or prove it? So I get an ice cream cone, and why not,
and carefully lick around the edges, a great tongue moon
lapping the ice cream planet, a great God tongue forming the ice cream mind,
like a thought moving around and around making sure nothing
drips out of the cosmic cone and down the cosmic arm
to fall on the pavement like the ghost of a half moon in the day sky.

Ashes Ashes

A man stumbles and looks back
at the bumpy walk, a woman veers
around a jumping dog, short steps
to get rebalanced, a child wumps
on its diapered bum, surprise-wide eyes,
viewing the world anew: these little teeters,
small struggles against gravity,
the emperor of the earthbound
against whose tyrannies
we've evolved this architecture,
a quiet revolt that we're not
dachshunded along the ground but rather
bold, gone skyward, head cloud high
like some risen thing.

Guide to Home Birth

What happens in a womb?
Ontogeny recapitulates phylogeny:
first you are a lizard, then you are a man.

Some days you think you have wings.
Sometimes you have gills and swim
everywhere through murky water.

Some days you gaze
through thin flesh, blinking
in the diffuse glare. There is doubt.

Once you enter the womb,
there is no going back. No matter
how long it takes, you come out.

Birth is spasmodic. There is
a violent peristalsis. Life comes
in a hiccup, a paroxysm.

In spite of your best intentions there are cries,
tears. For a long time,
you have no teeth.

Write Me a Letter

I try to mop up a spot on the tile only to find
the sun had spilled itself there momentarily and again
I've come to the place where words

fail me. Dante through all the circles found
something to say, as did the dead, when in life on Earth we're
stunned so frequently, mouth

agape, a stutter: light flaming bare trees, the kindness of a fellow,
inexplicable flicker of what seems like fate, and that
thing that atoms do when split

apart in time and space, wherever
they are: this instant
correspondence.

Insomniac Thoughts on the Special Theory of Relativity

Energy equals mass times the squared velocity of light in a vacuum.

My vacuum has a light
so I can clean in the dark.
I take on faith the results of my energy,
my constant motion, toward and away.

If $E = mc^2$ then I am
5,392,531,212,420,895,840 joules.
What potential.

Still, now, at my desk, I have no energy
to move from the leafy wave of morning,
desultory particles of birdsong.

What energy it takes to propel my desires,
how slowly they travel to light,
and how they drag the mass of me, toward and away.
Even at rest, I am a container of motion.

Subsume me, Dark Matter,
into the exquisite emptiness of your deep pocket.
Marry me with your endless ring.

Love and the Big Bang

As mass and energy are
two aspects of the same thing,
once you are gone, the solid
mass of you, furred chest,
your square fingernails,
the way your eyes are amused
long before your mouth is,
is there energy left?

And if energy
is of interest to energy,
then from no-thing but energy
may there arise a confluence,
a concentration resulting in mass—
and so are we reborn and universes
bang to being, expand
then collapse like vast seas to tide?

But your mispronunciations,
awkward dance moves and little songs,
and the nonmaterial not-brain that allows you
to be you and to consider such things—
is that also energy, to be neither created
nor destroyed, but to linger,
perseverative, humming
and forgetting?

Please remember me

Marie Curie 1867-1934

1.
This search to isolate isolates.
What drives you, woman, to melt
and weigh, melt and weigh,
distill yourself (a glorious poison)?
Great conflagration from

small flame. Late, and gaslight
licks the Paris night, cries
of paupers rise from the chilly *rue*,
across the way a pisser spies
the flame through the window,
thinks something's afire,

as she is,
bowing another hour
toward discovering the half-
life of love.

2.
I am held by a thousand bonds.
We were made to live together.
Now tell me, how am I going to manage to live.

We put you in the coffin Saturday morning.
I covered you with a few periwinkles from the garden.
I am held by a thousand bonds.

I am among those who think science has great beauty.
The beauty hurt me, and I lowered my veil.
Now tell me, how am I going to manage to live.

I work in the laboratory all day long; it is all I can do.
Whatever happens, even if one has to go on like a body without
    a soul, one must work just the same.
I am held by a thousand bonds.

It's possible we may succeed in preparing a greater quantity
    of the luckless substance.
Radium gave encouraging results: the epidermis, partially destroyed
    by its action, formed again in a healthy state.
(But tell me, how am I going to manage to live.)

Its luminosity cannot be seen by daylight but can easily be seen in half
    darkness.
(Your coffin was closed and I could see you no more.
It is the end of everything, everything, everything.)

I work in the laboratory all day long, it is all I can do.
Perhaps radium has something to do with these troubles, but it cannot be
    affirmed with certainty.
The luminosity can only be seen in half darkness.

In the laboratory, the evil has reached an acute stage.
I tried to make a measure for a graph on which you and I had each made
    several points, but I felt the impossibility of going on,
in the end. Everything, everything, everything

keeps me busy, housekeeping, the children, teaching and the laboratory,
    and I don't know how I shall manage it all.
Everybody talks. And I see you on your deathbed. The luminosity.
Perhaps beauty has something to do with these troubles. I cannot see.

I would like to dig into the ground somewhere to find a little peace.
I work, Pierre, in half darkness.
How will I manage everything, partially destroyed.

I am held by this luckless substance.
The luminosity cannot be seen.
It is the end of everything.
Tell me how to live.

3.
Her fingers are blackened. Pencils
all stubs. She recalls Pierre
as a murmur in the din, the clink of
others' glasses in a crowded room
where she can't eat enough nor
slake her own thirst.
Now in her shadowed home,
the dry November garden, she thinks
there is still so much to say.
I am still the girl running
home from school to trade
Russian crumbs for Polish water.

(Lines from section two were derived from letters and journal entries
quoted in *Madame Curie* by Eve Curie.)

The Orion Nebula

Whirling gases
catch Sun's light,
shimmying, turning,
pulsating like strobe.
And we too are vast
humming spaces of
tapdancing molecules and
pulse. What color
are we at the cellular level?
Does light penetrate our layers,
catch the edges of our atoms—do we
glow? When we die, burn out, do we
float away, fly skyward to join the astral hum?

Is my father up there somewhere,
the tobacco smell of him faint
on the edge of the Orion nebula?
Is Lila still on Earth in her kitchen,
twirling among the dust motes,
shining in the sun's slant?
Is there a great cloud of us rising now
with the steam from Sun burning
the sea-cold water off sodden
roofs, the glowing tar? Clearer
than smoke we rise.
How far will we go in the endless space,
or will we lie like sweat on the living,
beading on skin and shining?

Thoughts on Systems Theory

In a closed system,
things tend toward disorder,
dispersal. But nudge open the door,
let in some variables, and patterns
emerge. Things begin to hum
together, almost absently:
Build Me Up Buttercup? Or is it
the theme from Alfie? I worry
sometimes how long
it's taking us to merge
our nervous tapping into
something more like 4/4 time,
something like a pulse.

Wasp Nest

after Vallejo

Professor of nesting, teach us to adhere,
to mongrel, to creep in purpose, to suspend
with aplomb and be the center of desirous flying,
the center of love.

Rector of eaves, teach us to look down backwards
at the angry citizens always wanting entry, to refuse
the attentions of sky by hiding well
and shouldering the cloak of architecture.

Technician of wonder, teach us to travel by mud,
to house in humility, hum
without sound. We make you from our bodies
but you are more than we will ever be.
You build us to build you to build us to build you
in buildings you may outlast.

Professor of such little beauty.
Rector of refusal.
Technician of this short time.

IV. LE MOUVEMENT PERPÉTUEL

Found

There's a baby
in the crisped litter
of a roadside wood today, made pale
and lovely by an October snow.
Then even the skin is brittle.

It's never the big thing
but the fine and permeative that destroys
often beautifully. How are we a thing that hates
and is so hard to hate?

There's a boy
tucks a note into the pocket
of a coat he's sending a stranger, saying
"Have a good winter. Please write back."

A branch breaks, a lamp flickers,
the dog digs at a flash of something
paler than snow. A boy uncrinkles a note.
What happens next?

At Freeman's Farm

> *"...une meme vague depuis Troie roule sa hanche jusqu'a nous."*
> —Saint-John Perse
> *("... the same wave since Troy rolls its haunches toward us.")*

Men rise from the ranks of Joe Pye weed and loosestrife
ghostly as cow parsnip, weaving as waves
they come, tattered and white-ribbed, blooded
as the new sun. A Hessian gutters his final word,
falls back to bluettes and the undercurrent of voles.
Others stumble in tangled swirls of musket powder—
or is it veils of white pine pollen—in silence of morning,
heavy as a body, a body in arms;

    from a sea of Queen Anne's Lace like Poseidon's concubines,
    weed-draped, dripping, surging and stumbling as waves
    meet the beach with the cry of gulls on carrion,
    and some sink back to his bloody hands as
    behind them the sea explodes in gunmetal
    gray shards: noon hangs
    from the turret of an amphibious tank;

    to the sky as clouds of bees rise in black waves
    to some angry evening mission, intent like nectar a heady draw,
    their thrum the threat of oncoming storm.
    One group eases west, the other east,
    and land falls away under their enormous eyes.
    One rears, confused, cries like strangled metal,
    tail turning, toppling, wheels toward the trees' advance;

from the plain, vast, that slashes a horizon
with its waves of trench and scores summing
up ten hundreds, men crouched around tiny flames like fireflies
that light the night acrid and hissing. Mud,
mud, more mud, and blood. Earth's upturned
its guts and from it must have crawled
these creatures, their scattered gold carapaces, feathers;

   as a giant unfolds himself, parting heat as waves,
   towered, bilious, and even Earth's uncertain, even the sun
   blinks, mountains obscured, all the roses
   veiled, valleys afire, the heart of sands melts where no men
   rise but night to day. Mist.

Mimesis

We knew it from the savannah, blood
full from the lion's kill;

saw the apes bare teeth and cuff;
knew the effect of a chipped-off

flint or the hammered clubhead
in turning a moving body into spirit-fled

flesh; so it wasn't so far
when we wanted more

than our fair share of harvest,
or craved another man's woman's stout breasts.

But what was the first
scaped goat? When was it just

the incessant rasp of his breathing,
the annoying tendency of his borrowing

that made the one guy turn to another one
and bonk him with a handy bone?

A long tradition you follow, this Sunday morning.
Your neighbor fires up the leaf blower again.

Though he's a nice enough man, you imagine,
in great detail, beating him to death with the thing.

Afghani Pieta

> *In response to a photograph by Balazs Gardi:*
> *"Afghan man and wounded boy, Korengal Valley,*
> *Kunar Province, East Afghanistan, 2007"*

Eyes of the one holding the limp body,
the grainy surface as of stone,
or pigment made of rough powder.

The triolet: help sought
from the less of it, bonds
broken, things cut down.

There's a body.
There's a body
and there's life

left, it's seeping,
wounds we must look for
in tell-tale places.

There's the cradle:
the holder's arms,
chest to body.

The ache the eyes
are always turned toward:
the third figure obscure.

The matter is always
man. The suffering
old masters always knew.

The Human Equation

Let a = your neighbor The one with the pool and all the screaming kids and his incessant mowing, clipping, leaf blowing, and all the while blasting Billy Joel over everything else, and every Sunday evening his Aunt Millicent's mufflerless Ford.

Let b = a stranger Who forgot about the flame on the stove, and the sports page left on the counter, too close to the flame, and the grease in the frying pan from breakfast, all of which conflagrate so quickly that the man, who is upstairs taking a nap, wakes to choking smoke, and stumbles to the hallway, to the stairs, down the stairs partway but there is so much smoke, so much smoke that he stumbles, falls

If y = you,

consider that

$z = y(a) + y(b)$

if z = how you are able to hate wholeheartedly a, wish him ill, brood over your coffee cup at him out the kitchen window, snarl invective daily, and once drove right past him when his car was stuck in the snow that one year that was so bad, pretended you didn't even see him;

Yet,

one summer morning, driving to get the paper, hot, you saw the flame eating the house (b), pulled over quickly, ran from the car to the house, banged on the door, threw open the door to the beast of smoke, ducked inside calling, calling, heard b mumble from the darkness to the left, plunged forward, kicked his foot by mistake, grabbed at him, half dragged, half carried him out, as his cat shot through your legs, and you all gasped and choked in the smoking air.

(Does $b \neq a$?)

Solve for z.

Enemy's the Friend

after "David con la testa di Golia" by Caravaggio

That look on his face:
late night and a lot of beer
to wash down the shrooms,
moisten the smoke-logged throat,
and he's on politics and conspiracies.

He lost his head finally:
the day he freaked at what he thought
was helicopters approaching his healthy weed crop.
Then his own saner self held it up dripping,
that self small, pale, panting.
And he looked at himself with that same tenderness.

For don't we love our enemy?
When we mix our blood with theirs
it's a new and heady drink.
(And some days we suck it down
and cradle it to us as we're trying
one more time to stop.)

And now he's talking down addicts
from their bad heights, and his old head
hangs from the rearview mirror, always looking back.

Sunset Strip

The edges of overbuilt
LA are being buried
in mud and in the Philippines people are getting shot
for singing My Way
at karaoke
and somehow these seem connected, and not
a bad idea, like the Earth and we
are acting out
against the excess in ourselves, except
that's not how things work. Random,
from the French for gallop,
occurs to me
as February toward spring even as it succumbs
today to the wrest of winter,
a friend of a friend dead
slammed by the car of a fleeing robber
and the bouquet on the table losing its hues, bled
a bit by each day,
the hubris of everything's way.

Root Systems

Bittersweet sucks at the apples,
and the rest wanders
hungry underground.
I see it the next street
over and the next, all
one great growth,
tree and fence, your house, mine.
And water too, doesn't it
blanket the earth, a thirsty crust,
bonny coat all on and under?
Won't this stream I splash through
become the sea we cruise
in great yachts, then muddy
waste of Madagascar marsh,
the turgid Sunderbans?
And it rises to cloud to fall
again across all time,
so these drops once held
the hand of a man dead
in the bloody Ardennes,
cupped the sturdy skin
-boat of Saint Patrick. Oh, man,
we're never done with
each other and earth.
Take my tears for your tea.
Grind my teeth for your garden.
Let me feed your child's child.
Let him suck
the bitter root sweet.

V. PROBLEMS AND AFFINITIES

Burning Bush

The Genome Project guy thinks God works
in deoxyribonucleic acid
His wonder to behold.

My neighbor mutters to her grocery bag;
its tattered handle hangs
on her every word.

Deep underground
scientists smash atoms
to read the leavings.

I gaze down
the arced
throats of iris.

How we parse this profane world,
find smaller, smaller
sacraments,

holy fire,
spiral of smoke
from which we can't avert our eyes—

Lost

*In the zoo's amphibious tanks' blueglow curved
half hidden things dark dim dark dim*

Kierkegaard said that we are two
selves divided, one divine, one sullied
by its reflection in the group;

*I look up no one I recognize I am
eight years old and my group has disappeared*

to try to see the self in others
is despair, but despair is the beginning
of the shadowed path toward God.

*Run to the open doors run through the bucking storm
where's my group I cry no one no self to find myself*

And who are we without each other,
sweat-smelling, shuffling,
God so far away and flickering?
dark dim dark dim dark

Psalm: It Is Dark

It is dark here. My eyes are
useless. Grace may be this way. I don't know.
I am no seedling.

I push against dirt, rock,
my fingers rake, nails crack.
I am no mole with troweling feet.

Pressed against tangled root
I thrash and fumble.
I am no earthworm.

What should I do with these limbs,
this head, a tongue?
Why was I given them?

There is strange water coursing here.
There is fire. I feel a great trembling.

Lac du Saint Sacrament

Muscled bulk of ice backed through here,
shard-sharp elbows and blood-pocked granite
fingers, reached into your own guts
to pull icy fronds of underground streams
and I waist myself in it, wear this

world a wedding gown, a shroud. This
is my body, visible sign of invisible
reality. You dissolve me:
earth's impulsive intentions,
its inadvertent and slow evolving violence.
You are a rugged means of grace.

Eve, Looking Back

How the body remembers:
sudden plunge of stomach

feet chill
hands chill

eyes wide
with what you've done, how

recklessly you used your
tongue, what

hunger
you revealed in

the ready parting
of your lips

Hieroglyphs

Why do you write in restless cursive across the sky? You
etch runes on my winter windows. Here are the stars
again that seem to hold some
secret if I could get close enough to hear.
Must I strain to know your intentions?
Others murmur incantations. Others search
for patterns. I am mute and running
to signs I can't understand—a hawk
in my backyard hunting small birds, a curtain
of sun sifting through cloud to illuminate one
mountain—or digging the garden for a Rosetta stone.

Within Without

Oh, God, I am not the cedar roots passion-thatched
    to soil and stone.
I am no catalpa's limbs flung wide to receive.
Not the cardinal who calls each morning, crimson
    through shattered garden and hedgerow.
I am not the thirsty earth, nor stench of rising
    swamp, its furled skunk cabbage and mud.
Not the purposeful wind. Not the elaborate trace of
    caddis fly larva splayed on mica-sparked rock.
God, if I am you, we are less than feather.
We are wanton. Flotsam.
We are the laceless lost shoe, a broken comb, the crumpled
    note on the grassy verge.
We are gutter mash. Chaff.
God, if you are me, we are lost. We have forgotten
    what we're here for.
God, if we are one, who will I ask?

Ode to Nevelson in Spring

Glimpse	Cut that out:	registers
the	o	like
c	n	phys
u	e	i
r	light's	c
v	ap-	a
e'	ple	l
s	glare	pain.
oeuvre	L	So
that	o	does the
a	n	"s
l	e	e
e	l	l
r	i	f
t	n	of you
bud	e	…
muscle.	ss	prime mover."

Signs of Passerines

I try not to think. All the things I've left behind.
My name on a white page, clack of my words clattering down.
The window: taking it apart. The center.
I did not have to throw all
my belongings in a box.
(Only small dreams.)
The god of wisdom is the patron of
metalsmiths, musicians, and sailors.
Beauty's long etymology tells us only
that we've long thought the lovely good:
small though it will be in poetry form:
gratitude pressed thin and broad like a sail.

A Matter of Spirit and Flesh

I read it as "a matter of spirit and
fish," and think, yes,
spirit is undulant, pulled
by the moon's moods,
a body's impulse,
at once vast and intimate
as a hand under a blouse.

And we're helpless,
lifted and taken, our flesh
held in it and its breath
ours, its plunge
our terror, the way
its scales splinter light
our erratic dance, as if

we were finned, as if
in this medium, nothing
is without grace.

Spring on Lacy Road

As the sun shifts   so light slides from what was
            the land too offers new angles,
once a scythe's   the shallow scoop of a salt
            curve on the col's lip to a spoon,
cellar, and the col's   a curled palm spread to read.
            shadow's now ripened and ripening,

Refuting Buddha

Even in the
is-ness of all things—
snow doused rut,
bleak skeleton of blackberry—
there is a waiting:
water of what's next,
small fist of intent.
Who can live in the moment
amid all this soon-to-be:
bud of laurel,
aspen's catkin, thirst
of the dirt road?

VI. ENTR'ACTE

Appointment With

Here we are, Hercule, at another
country estate, another body
in a room locked

from the inside. Another well dressed widow weeps
conspicuously in the parlor comforted by a handsome young
man of vague origin.

The victim's brother stares
out a window in the study. We all heard the violent quarrel over
their father's will.

And there seems to be some history
between the victim and
Miss Templeton, the librarian from Tunbridge Wells.

But just once, Hercule, let's not
interview the servants. Let's not examine the glass by the
bedside. This time, let's let the tuft of blue wool under the victim's

fingernail be. Here at the breakfast table shrouded
in white damask, panicle
of lilac in a slender vase, startle of red

raspberry jam on the edge of a gilt
-trimmed plate, pour me another cup. Let's
lean against the flocked curtains noosed

with gold cords, watch the deer ease
across the far field. Just once, my dear Poirot, let's live
for a time in the mystery.

Memory of a Voyage (Magritte)

Soft the stone
light of rigid past
unbattered though
it peels, the i-
mage, and cracks
and if the smell's gone
damp, cellared, and color
has clayed, the re-
collection of the recoll-
ection is clear
as the lines that frame
the frame of the
photo on the wall.

ABOUT THE WORD WORKS

The Word Works, a nonprofit literary organization, publishes contemporary poetry collections and presents public programs. Since 1981, the organization has sponsored the Washington Prize, a monetary award and book publication, to an American or Canadian poet. Monthly, The Word Works offers free literary programs in the Chevy Chase, MD, Café Muse series, and each summer, it holds free poetry programs in Washington, DC's Rock Creek Park. Annually in June, two high school students debut in the Joaquin Miller Series as winners of the Jacklyn Potter Young Poets Competition. Other programs have included workshops, master classes, symposia, international artist retreats, panel discussions, and archival projects with prominent American poets.

As a 501(c)3 organization, The Word Works has received awards from the National Endowment for the Arts, National Endowment for the Humanities, DC Commission on the Arts & Humanities, Witter Bynner Foundation, Poets & Writers, The Writer's Center, Bell Atlantic, the David G. Taft Foundation, and others, including many generous private patrons. The Word Works has established an archive of artistic and administrative materials in the Washington Writing Archive housed in the George Washington University Gelman Library. The Word Works is a member of the Council of Literary Magazines and Presses and distributed by Small Press Distribution.

More information at wordworksbooks.org

ABOUT THE HILARY THAM CAPITAL COLLECTION

The Hilary Tham Capital Collection (HTCC) is an imprint of The Word Works featuring poets who assist this nonprofit in its mission to promote contemporary poetry. Judge Gray Jacobik selected the 2011 HTCC book.

In 1989, Hilary Tham was the first author published in the Capital Collection imprint. In 1994, when she became Word Works Editor-in-Chief, she revitalized and expanded the imprint. Tham died in 2005 and the imprint was renamed in her honor.

THE HILARY THAM CAPITAL COLLECTION:

Mel Belin, *Flesh That Was Chrysalis*, 1999
Doris Brody, *Judging the Distance*, 2001
Sarah Browning, *Whiskey in the Garden of Eden*, 2007, 2nd printing 2011
Grace Cavalieri, *Pinecrest Rest Haven*, 1998
Christopher Conlon, *Gilbert and Garbo in Love*, 2003
    Mary Falls: Requiem for Mrs. Surratt, 2007
Donna Denizé, *Broken like Job*, 2005
W. Perry Epes, *Nothing Happened*, 2010
James Hopkins, *Eight Pale Women*, 2003
Brandon Johnson, *Love's Skin*, 2006
Marilyn McCabe, *Perpetual Motion*, 2012
Judith McCombs, *The Habit of Fire*, 2005
James McEwen, *Snake Country*, 1990
Miles David Moore, *The Bears of Paris*, 1995
    Rollercoaster, 2004
Kathi Morrison-Taylor, *By the Nest*, 2009
Michael Schaffner, *The Good Opinion of Squirrels*, 1996
Maria Terrone, *The Bodies We Were Loaned*, 2002
Hilary Tham, *Bad Names for Women*, 1989
    Counting, 2000
Barbara Ungar, *Charlotte Brontë, You Ruined My Life*, 2011
Jonathan Vaile, *Blue Cowboy*, 2005
Rosemary Winslow, *Green Bodies*, 2007
Michele Wolf, *Immersion*, 2011

ALSO FROM THE WORD WORKS

WASHINGTON PRIZE BOOKS

Nathalie F. Anderson, *Following Fred Astaire*, 1998
Michael Atkinson, *One Hundred Children Waiting for a Train*, 2001
Carrie Bennett, *biography of water*, 2004
Peter Blair, *Last Heat*, 1999
Richard Carr, *Ace*, 2008
Ann Rae Jonas, *A Diamond Is Hard but Not Tough*, 1997
Frannie Lindsay, *Mayweed*, 2009
Richard Lyons, *Fleur Carnivore*, 2005
Fred Marchant, *Tipping Point*, 1993, 3rd printing 1999
Ron Mohring, *Survivable World*, 2003
Brad Richard, *Motion Studies*, 2010
Jay Rogoff, *The Cutoff*, 1994
Prartho Sereno, *Call from Paris*, 2007
Enid Shomer, *Stalking the Florida Panther*, 1987, 2nd edition 1993
John Surowiecki, *The Hat City after Men Stopped Wearing Hats*, 2006
Miles Waggener, *Phoenix Suites*, 2002
Mike White, *How to Make a Bird with Two Hands*, 2011
Nancy White, *Sun, Moon, Salt*, 1992, 2nd edition 2010

INTERNATIONAL EDITIONS

Yoko Danno & James C. Hopkins, *The Blue Door*
Moshe Dor, *Scorched by the Sun*. Translated by Barbara Goldberg
Moshe Dor, Barbara Goldberg, Giora Leshem, eds., *The Stones Remember*
Myong-Hee Kim, *Crow's Eye View: The Infamy of Lee Sang, Korean Poet*
Vladimir Levchev, *Black Book of the Endangered Species*

ADDITIONAL TITLES

Karren L. Alenier, *Wandering on the Outside*
Karren L. Alenier, Hilary Tham, Miles David Moore, eds.,
    Winners: A Retrospective of the Washington Prize
Christopher Bursk, *Cool Fire*
Barbara Goldberg, *Berta Broadfoot and Pepin the Short*
Jacklyn Potter, Dwaine Rieves, Gary Stein, eds.,
    Cabin Fever: Poets at Joaquin Miller's Cabin
Robert Sargent, *Aspects of a Southern Story*
    A Woman from Memphis

ABOUT THE AUTHOR

Marilyn McCabe's work has been published in a variety of literary magazines, including *Painted Bride Quarterly, Nimrod, Beloit Poetry Journal*, and *Rhino*, and she has received awards through the New York State Council on the Arts and the Adirondack Center for Writing. Her chapbook *Rugged Means of Grace* was published by Finishing Line Press in 2011. She earned an MFA in poetry from New England College. marilynmccabe.net

ABOUT THE ARTISTS

The ParkeHarrisons construct fantasies in the guise of environmental performances for the protagonists of their images. The artists combine elaborate sets within vast landscapes to address issues surrounding man's relationship to the earth and technology while additionally delving into the human condition.

www.ingramcontent.com/pod-product-compliance
Lightning Source LLC
Chambersburg PA
CBHW020957090426
42736CB00010B/1363